The Little Book To Salvage Self-Esteem

Denisia Hockley

PREFACE

We know that the first 4 or so years of life profoundly shape our emotional and relational circuits. The last decade has seen an explosion in the field of developmental neuroscience, its intersections with attachment dynamics, and its impact on how we nurture children (the fundamental starting point of every person). Professionals like Dan Seigal and Allan Schore come to mind. Yet there is another level, we also know intuitively that every 'good enough' mother (to use Winnicott's practical term) somehow manages to come through with the goods, even if she has never read a word of Dan Seigal. The Little Book Series (in particular Your Child the Little Scientist) values developmental science that confirms the nature and shape of "good enough" nurturance BUT deviates from typical ways of teaching so as to avoid getting lost in technical detail. The Amazing Abilities of Your Magical Mind goes even further by taking cutting edge scientific thinking and presenting concepts that are both exciting and challenging to your belief system.

The Little Book
To
Salvage
Self-Esteem

Oh No! Not another
'Self Esteem' Book

I will keep this short, entertaining and to the point; since there are trillions of self-esteem books out there; and I don't want you falling asleep while reading this one.

Contents

Introduction

Self–esteem, self-image, self-efficacy: How do you see yourself? Feel about your 'Self'? Evaluate your abilities? You would think the one common denominator within these concepts would be your 'Self'........right????????

You have grown up believing that it is wrong to be 'self-ish' and probably good to be 'self-sacrificing'
To answer the question above...The constant is OPOs (Other peoples' opinions) yup, at the end of the day that is pretty much what drives you and most of the issues that haunt you!

Your 'Self' is your core; it is the motor that drives you! it is informed by your thoughts and feelings; your experiences are important BUT your interpretations and evaluations of them ARE way more so! Why would you want to 'sacrifice' your 'Self' because you certainly are of no benefit to anyone without it!
Self...ish ? ...Approval?

Being self-ish: Now I obviously don't mean selfish like the moron who put their needs in front of mine by stealing my sandals from the beach the other day! But you do have to put your legitimate needs first; if I have a dollar and I give it to a homeless man that is not helpful, it's stupid! Far better I use the dollar to help myself then I can make $50 and give one to each of ten.

People often enjoy a martyr complex… in that they feel good if they go without; that's ok if you're going without a trip to the Bermudas, or a new car, so that you can help someone; but depleting your necessary resources, especially physical, emotional and psychological, means you will again end up with nothing left to give.

Feeding, nurturing and supporting yourself so that you are a stronger more confident person means that the people around you will benefit just by you being in their space! Before you go out and help the world you need to retreat and develop a strong, healthy and complete 'Self'

Confidence is the most attractive trait possible! If you don't like yourself why should anyone else!

So about those OPOs: You can say you don't care what others think, but you do! We all do! How much though, does it influence or even control your everyday life, your choices, and your self-evaluation? Seriously, what makes you think others are really that interested in your stuff anyway!

When you walk along the beach and you're 'people-watching', are you having thoughts like…'she should not be wearing that…' 'he's hot' OMG she's fat'??? Yup, you probably are! Is that about the people you are watching or is it about you? As long as you keep it to yourself (keep your mouth shut) who cares? who is affected?

Is it right? Not always! Is it human? Yes! It is a typical human failing, most people do it at some time or other and as wrong as it is, it is harmless to everyone except the person thinking it. Next time you catch yourself you might like to re-think your use of that mind-space and those little energy tokens (see The Little Book to Annihilate Anxiety). Don't get too bent over it though; as I said, a typical human trait everyone is guilty of!

Aside from the above example, people generally are NOT watching you, judging you or even thinking about you: Most of the time they are doing exactly the same as you are…. thinking about themselves and their own stuff. Most of the time you are not even registering on their radar!

In terms of what counts though, the things where you stress over OPOs are important in as much as you are feeding your own need for approval, fear of rejection, and basically saying that in order to be of value everyone must like everything you do and everything you are. Even if that were important it would never be possible; maybe in an alternate universe where everything is the same color size shape etc.; where everything is a clone of everything else and there are zero differences…eewwww how boring!

So let us start with physical appearance because low self-image always seems to include a huge element of hating how we look. Pretty people are always getting dumped for someone less fortunate looking. Go figure… maybe external appearances are not everything to everyone. Try not to compare yourself with others: if you really must, then at least look both ways!

How you see yourself physically is largely determined by

your own insecurities and self-esteem (different from, but closely related to self-image). I remember about 15 years ago, I was somewhat larger but quite confident most of the time. I went out one night full of bubble and quite sure I looked hot… anyway it was a great night, met a nice guy, all of that. A couple months later I went out in the same outfit, same weight, pretty much a clone of that night: only difference was my self-esteem was very low and I was convinced that I was fat as a cow and a total f'ugly (good old hindsight). The point to the story is; two separate occasions when a person's physical appearance is virtually identical can have completely opposite outcomes because of confidence (self-esteem) levels. Even what you see in the mirror can be affected. I am somewhat fascinated by the way a brain can even tell your eyeballs to see things differently depending on what else is going on in your head.

We have all seen current affairs programs featuring an anorexic person who looks like the walking dead with bones protruding through what's left of their flesh; and yet when these people look in the mirror they still see fat. As bad as that is, it is kinda intriguing that your brain is so powerful it can lie to your eyes!

So many of your problems are caused by your amazing brain which is really cool because you can learn to understand and harness that power to work 'for you' instead of against you (see Amazing Abilities of Your Magical Mind)

Sometimes I try to be like other people
But it gets boring So I go back to being me!

There is nothing wrong with making effort to look your best, taking care of your skin, body etc., a degree of vanity is, again, human; just do not fall into the trap of thinking that your looks are your identity, that how you look determines whether you will be loved or rejected. Most of the rejection you feel actually comes from yourself (originally there were other sources but these days it's mostly you and what is on your hard-drive).

The 'Little Book to be Physically Phabulous' goes into how you can learn to be, look and feel healthy and 'attractive' on all levels. But I do need to make a mention now in regards to weight: It is fine to be big and beautiful BUT a walking heart attack, being so big you cannot breath, move or live any kind of normal life AND making your kids obese is NOT OK! Be as big as you like as long as you are *genuinely* healthy, happy and enjoying the life you and your kids deserve.

Obesity is often a sign of low self-esteem, it's not a choice or a lifestyle; they are just excuses for not taking control of your life and respecting your right to happiness. More often than not people are obese by choice! (In a rather latent dysfunctional way).

Back to people-watching for a second... have you really looked at the human species? Seriously? We are not that aesthetically pleasing. In fact of all the creatures on this planet we are one of the weirdest looking. It's like all the artistry and engineering went into creating all the animals on the earth and we are made up of the left overs. For me cane toads and big hairy spiders are the only species less attractive than humans, oh, and cockroaches. But hey, you can have a different opinion if you like.. We did however score the 'brain' although that also creates a serious debate, in terms of ability to use it properly!

You never see a tiger worrying about a zit

Or a tortoise complaining about wrinkles

And who would want to change a baby orangutan's hairdo

Self-esteem and self-image are reasonably well understood but what about self-efficacy? How you see your abilities/capacities to achieve success/ results at whatever it is you need to do. One thing is for sure, if you put enough energy into believing you will fail you probably will. So put that same amount of energy into believing you can do what you want to do and be what you want to be and chances are you will succeed.

What do you have to lose by trying; we have already established that you're running some pretty powerful software in that computer you call your brain. We just need to clean out the viruses and negative programs and maybe update some of that destructive crap on your hard-drive.

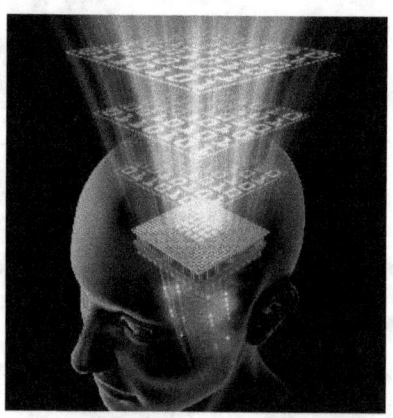

Pathological Critic –v- Healthy Voice

You have a negative inner voice that attacks and judges you! We all have one, but people with low self-esteem seem to take more notice of theirs!

Your critic blames you for everything that goes wrong! Reminds you of every mistake you ever made. Compares you with others! Keeps record of your 'failures' so that it can keep reminding you…just in case your self-esteem should start improving - it can bring you back to earth! Sometimes it sounds like your friend, telling you to be the best, do your best; don't concede defeat…because if you don't win you are worthless!! Nothing!! A failure!!

Your critic is a mind reader too, it tells you what other people are thinking about you…like you are ugly or stupid or annoying to be around… Your critic exaggerates…you are ALWAYS late; you NEVER have any friends…This critic is so good at controlling your thoughts and your self-esteem that you don't even notice it there half the time…

Your healthy voice may have gotten tired of arguing with your critic, it may have gone to sleep on you…you need to encourage it to come out again… It says things like…'check and see if you are blowing things out of proportion???' 'Is it possible you are being too hard on yourself?'

- It wants to challenge the critic! Where is the evidence?
- It wants to look at other ways of interpreting the situation!
- It wants to identify and change some of your old beliefs about yourself!

Sometimes a person appears to have a good self-esteem...but what you don't know is that it may revolve solely around achievement or maybe one particular area of their life. Someone you know may seem to have a good self-esteem; perhaps they spend all their life either at work or asleep... because they feel good about their working self, but not about themselves as an individual (i.e.: when they are not wearing an identity hat).

A high achiever can have a low self-esteem because (IN THEIR MIND) they are only as good as their last race.

It is ok NOT to be perfect!!!! (Even if such a mythical concept were even possible) It is ok to be AVERAGE!!!! (Which we all are anyway)

Want to be outstanding but afraid to stand out?

If you lack confidence and/or self-esteem...engage in confidence building activities: Get Active physically, mentally and emotionally!

GIVE YOURSELF CREDIT, POSITIVE
REINFORCEMENT WORKS WONDERS!

Allow yourself to be YOU
Allow yourself to make mistakes

It is ok to be wrong!!!!!
Build up your self-esteem (if others won't tell you how good you are ... TELL YOURSELF

Everyone has some good qualities (even if they are hard to find). Find yours! Express your feelings and thoughts ASSERTIVELY & APPROPRIATELY

DO WHAT YOU CAN PLUS A TINY BIT MORE!

Catch yourself when you start to assume your negative emotions reflect the way things really are!

Let go of the need to be right all the time, to never make a mistake, to be perfect. These things are impossible anyway!

The consequence of setting these impossible standards is that you develop guilt when you fall short and develop anger/frustration with yourself.

Do Not Live Down to Your Own Expectations!

The irony is that living down to your self-expectations can give you a dysfunctional kind of satisfaction because you have reinforced your core beliefs of being useless, worthless and/or a failure. And the world according to your hard-drive makes sense!

Instead or living down to those faulty beliefs you need to become aware of what they are, challenge them and replace them with realistic, factual ones.

People with low self-esteem often assume everyone else is better, smarter etc. etc. Recognize that many of your thoughts are not facts. They are merely assumptions, which determine how you feel and what you do.

Before you can experience any event, you must process it with your mind and give it meaning. You must understand what is happening to you before you can feel it. Therefore it is not the actual events that cause you distress, but your perceptions/ interpretations that inform your choices; insight develops when you start to really listen to your thoughts: your healthy voice and your pathological critic.

Challenge the evidence. Develop awareness in terms of the origin of those core belief – ones like 'I need to be liked by everyone or 'I am worthless' and anything that involves statements about 'everyone' 'no-one' 'must' 'can't'. Start to replace those beliefs with something more reasonable and rational like – 'It would be cool to be liked by everyone but sometimes this is not possible and my worth should not depend on it'.

If a lot of your irrational thoughts are similar, it may mean that there is a common core belief responsible for these irrational thoughts. Dig around and see where/who it originated from.

Once you have done this ask yourself how your behavior and feelings will change with your new rational responses, compared to believing in your core irrational beliefs: especially the one that revolve around judging, blaming and putting you, or anyone else down.

Put together a list of positive thoughts, especially ones that focus on your good qualities. Write them onto small cards and put them in your purse or wallet or pocket (or that smartphone you carry everywhere) every hour take a few moments to read them. Have you been thinking like this in the past hour, or thinking the usual negative stuff? You may want to repeat the thought 10-20 times, and then replace the card/message. You may also add blank cards, which means you have to spend the next 60 seconds thinking supportively.

If you do what you have always done you will get what you have always got!

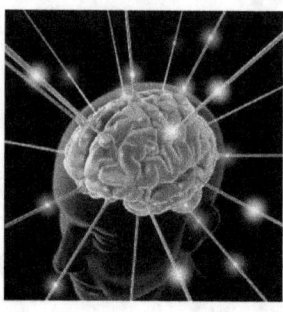

Awareness: Thought catching – by firstly identifying your triggers or cues you will start to identify the thinking that result in your distress.

Remember, in order to catch your thoughts you need to acknowledge negative feelings such as guilt, key words or phrases such as 'must' and 'should', things you avoid/put off doing as well as unpleasant body sensations that go with fear/ anxiety.

- Examine the evidence
- Find alternative explanations
- De-catastrophize
- Examine the advantages and disadvantages of thinking this way
- Rational responses
- Writing your journal

STOP thinking that others are always more right or more important!

Before you can have a relationship with anyone you need to develop a healthy relationship with you! Do you judge, blame, put down or straight up insult anyone else the way you do to you?

It's OK to be wrong!

More Personal Rights

I have the right to be wrong
I have the right to make mistakes
I have the right to be average
I have the right to like myself just the way I am
I have the right to have faults and imperfections
I have the right to learn from my past
I have the right to grow and evolve
I have the right to admit when I screw up
I have the right to screw up

I have the right to take as long as it takes to get to know myself
I have the right to not be liked by everyone
I have the right to fail sometimes

I want to do most things well most of the time. Like everyone, I will occasionally fail or make a mistake. I can cope with that, and I can choose to take constructive steps to do better next time. Being personally successful means doing my best, not beating others. It is disappointing when things aren't how I would like them to be but I can cope with that. Usually I can take constructive steps to make things more as I would like them to be. But if I can't, it doesn't help me to exaggerate my disappointment.

Your problem(s) may be influenced by factors outside your control but your thoughts and actions also influence your problem(s) and they **are** in your control.

Worrying about something that **might** go wrong won't stop it from happening. It just makes you unhappy now. You can take constructive steps to prepare for possible problems and that's as much as anyone can do.

Facing difficult situations may make you feel bad at the time but you can cope with that. Putting off problems doesn't make them any easier; it just gives you longer to worry about them.

It's good to get support from others when you want it but the only person you really need to rely on is you. At the end of the day you are just as capable as anyone else. Do not assume other people's advice is always better than your own.

Your problem(s) may have started in some past event but what keeps it (them) going now are your thoughts and actions and they are under your control.

You no longer see people as either good or bad; things as either perfect or disastrous; yourself as either weak, incompetent or an idiot. The world is rarely black or white and this sort of thinking leaves no room for mistakes or for just being average /human.

Do not only compare yourself to other people that are more successful than you see yourself. Do develop a more balanced perspective on people and events.

Learn to accept compliments even if you do not agree; all you need to say is 'thank you' even if the compliment is obviously incorrect (someone says you look great when you hobble out of hospital after extreme surgery). Fact is, even if you do not look great, clearly the person has the intent of making you feel good, and isn't that an even better gift than just observing your physicality.

Allow yourself to feel pride in your abilities and achievements and realize that you play a part in creating opportunities and pleasant experiences

Find something to positively reinforce about yourself on a daily basis

If you blow one job interview because of nerves an overgeneralizing thought could be 'I never succeed in job interviews' (replace with: I didn't succeed in this one, I'll keep trying until I do). Develop a balanced perspective: Talk to yourself about your negative thoughts, be specific rather than general about why you are unhappy with who you are.

It is fair to say that **all** of my clients, over many years, have or have had, self-esteem issues; I don't know the stats but I would bet that after diet books there are more self-esteem books written than on any other topic.

Of all the times that I have asked a self-hater to think of someone with whom they would happily exchange their mind, body and soul (the whole package): Every one of them has ultimately decided they would rather keep themselves. Interesting!

Worry –vs-
Positive Self-Talk

When faced with a daunting task or issue you really need to process and plan!

'What is it I have to do?'   Develop a plan to deal with it. Think about how you can prepare. Planning is better than getting anxious (fearful). 'Don't worry. Worry won't help anything'. Of course it is easier to say than to do…. Worry is a habit! When you catch yourself worrying push yourself into a solution focused mind state.

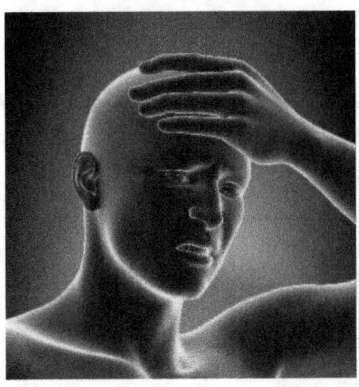

If worry were a productive process everyone would be extremely successful – given that worrying is something most people are really good at. Maybe what you think is anxiety, is eagerness to confront the stressor (anxiety and excitement have the exact same physiological symptoms in your body)

Throughout a stressful event pace yourself: 'One step at a

time'. Keep reminding yourself that you can meet this challenge and do the best you can' 'Psych' yourself up. You can convince yourself to do it. Don't think fear, just focus on what you have to do. Stay focused on the small picture. If you don't get it 100% right what is the worst that can happen? Will anyone die? What are your choices?

When feelings of fear come, tell yourself to 'pause'. What is it you have to do? Breathe! Don't try to eliminate your fear totally. It may represent performance stress. Keep it manageable. Reinforce yourself with 'It worked. I did it. It wasn't that bad after all'

Is it possible that you made more out of the fear than it was worth? Every time you adopt this attitude/process your core beliefs regarding your self-efficacy change a little! Success breeds success! We are not talking about the success of the actual task, No, the success at you facing challenges regardless of outcomes!

Learn to be pleased with any progress you have made.

Not freaking out is an achievement!

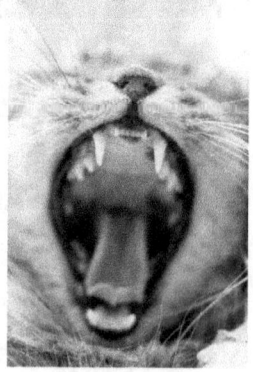

You have little control over many things in life – other people's behavior, the weather, politics and the economy. But! As difficult as it seems…we can choose whether or not to dwell on how UNFAIR life is and how it shouldn't have happened 'to me' OR we can focus on doing everything we possibly can to increase our chances of becoming self-confident and improving our personal circumstances.

Feeling helpless is another component of poor self-efficacy! When you see the cause of helplessness as universal it means that you think that there's pretty much no point in anything, nothing you do matters at the end of the day. The why-bother-we're-all-going-to-die anyway school of thought. When you see the cause of helplessness as personal then it is perceived to be because you're not strong or smart or capable or healthy enough.

Helplessness can be seen as due to a specific cause ('I can't get a girlfriend because I'm bald').

Helplessness can be seen as being due to a transient cause ('I can't concentrate because I have got a headache') or a permanent cause ('my memory is terrible').

Try interpreting your helplessness in ways that are more specific and transient and you'll start noticing some of the things that you could have more control over.

If you don't think you are worth it, who will?

THERE IS ONLY ONE PERSON WHO CAN CHANGE THE WAY YOU FEEL ABOUT YOURSELF! As psychologists we will tell you that you cannot get your self-esteem from others; and this is true because if the woman in your life gave you what you need to like yourself then she can also take it away!

Truth is we all do, to some extent, gauge our worth on the responses and reactions of others, it's pretty normal but just be aware of it: Make sure the primary source of your confidence and self-evaluation comes from you!

YOU ARE MOSTLY ONLY LIMITED BY WHAT YOU BELIEVE TO BE POSSIBLE!!!

People adopt beliefs which impact on their self-esteem. Such as;

•   I must prove that I am worthwhile through my

achievements
- I must do things perfectly or not at all
- I must have everyone's approval all the time
- I need to be loved by someone in order to be worthwhile
- The world must be fair and just

How will you know when you are 'Good Enough?'

Self-esteem based solely on achievements

Many people attempt to build self-esteem through their achievements. External factors can be a great source of self-esteem but ultimately it's the internal factors that are most important. If you learn to derive your good feelings about yourself only from material things and/or what others say, then if the material things vanish and others treat you negatively, you may feel helpless to generate any positive feelings.

People, who base their self-esteem only on the things they do, put themselves under great pressures as they attempt to get through an endless list of accomplishments. The striving becomes the goal and they are never satisfied.

They miss the chance to stop and feel good about what they have already done. You are a person who is trying to live the best way you know how. You are as worthwhile as every other person! We all have faults (and lots of good stuff too). Whatever you do, whatever you contribute should not come from the need to prove your value but from you being the real and authentic you. Look for a balance of achievement, relationships and leisure activities/ goals; this is important to our psychological wellbeing.

Striving for Perfection: You may be saying, what's wrong with high standards and of course there is nothing wrong with high standards. What IS wrong is that you say 'I am not good enough unless I reach those high standards'. Your productivity and sense of achievement are enhanced when you aim to do things well. This is very different from having to do well. The former brings satisfaction, but the latter leads to temporary relief followed by frustration at having to achieve such high standards again (and again and again). People who attempt to do things perfectly are often motivated by the belief that this is what others expect and their efforts are seen as a major way of getting approval. You continually raise the bar, making it impossible to ever be good enough.

'Love me just the way I am'

Disadvantages of perfectionism include:

- Loneliness due to fear of criticism (social anxiety)
- Decreased productivity
- Troubled personal relationships
- Low self-esteem
- Vulnerability to depression
- Performance anxiety
- Obsessive-compulsive problems

Ask yourself:

- What are the advantages of setting such high standards?
- If you aim for perfection, how do you know when you get there?
- Who actually told you that you had to be perfect?
- Do you even know of a 'perfect' person?

Learn to recognize when your expectations (or the expectations of others) are unrealistic and remind yourself that you do not have to agree with them.

Become aware that you do not become more valued by doing things 'perfectly'; you just become more overworked and frustrated (and possibly rather annoying).

Regard mistakes as opportunities to learn. Learn to enjoy your experiences in the present rather than being preoccupied with the end result. Paradoxically, one significant way of improving your performance involves lowering your standards.

Instead of aiming for 100% all of the time, try aiming for 70% or 50%. If you attempt to do reasonably well and to enjoy yourself at the same time, then you are more likely to relax. If you focus on more than just the standard of your performance you may also obtain more satisfaction from the activity.

Test out, for yourself, whether you have to do things perfectly in order to achieve satisfaction.

Self-esteem based on the approval of others: The need for approval begins with the message received in your early years from your family and other significant people. For example 'You must do as you are told in order to gain our approval'. If you have poor self-esteem then you'll probably view yourself through other people's eyes. This leads you to become too dependent on the praise, opinions and the comments of others; because you believe that your own judgments do not count. You will also be vulnerable to others by letting their attitudes and mood influence your feelings and behaviors.

How painful is it when you overhear people making a social arrangement that you are not invited to...someone's birthday party or drinks after work...You take it personally, well who wouldn't...what other explanation can you come up with other than' no one likes you'?

Perhaps well-meaning parents did everything for you. They didn't even realize that you interpreted this to mean you were too useless to do things yourself.

How to handle criticism: (stop and think: sometimes no matter how badly the criticism is delivered it may be partly true? It may be something you can take on board and benefit from?) Recognize that your worth is not completely based on what you do. Remember that people's judgments about your behaviors are only their opinions, which may or may not be valid (who made them the expert on................?)

Consider alternate ways of handling criticism: Avoid exaggerating or magnifying the incident. Don't jump straight into denial or defensiveness! As I said, listen first, it may even be ultimately rewarding.

I am not better, I am just different'

Relationships, Rejection & other Facts of Life!

- Challenge your thinking first: There are times when you have rejected people; not because of anything bad about them, but because of your own needs or desires at that time!
- Remember that rejection fired by anger may be temporary

- Recognize that not everyone will like you. Do you like everyone you meet? Be real!

- Falling out with a particular person does not mean that you will not have other satisfying relationships in the future

- Remind yourself that you will eventually get over the anger and disappointment. Don't build it up into a catastrophe

- Remember that the person is not rejecting all of you, just some of your behavior.

Problems in relationships can occur for many reasons (see The Little Book to Revive Relationships). Don't over simplify the situation by blaming yourself or the other person. Consider what you can learn. Are there some characteristics in yourself you would like to change to improve your relationship (s), especially the relationship with YOU?

It is important to be able to reject others as well as learning to cope with rejection. If you have difficulty saying 'no' it is probably hard for you to accept 'no' from others. As you become more comfortable saying 'no' it will become easier to accept this from others. Be careful to avoid reading more into the situation than was intended.

'I'm gonna hold my breath till you say I am OK'

Learn to laugh at yourself!

Primary concepts to think about

- Other people's responses and reactions
- Energy/Motivation/Activity
- RELAXATION…brain rhythms (see Magical Mind & Annihilate Anxiety))
- THOUGHTS   THINKING STYLES ATTITUDES & BELIEFS
- 'Blueprints' 'inner programs' 'your hard drive'
- Choices
- If you do what you have always done you will get what you have always got!!
- No person or situation can MAKE you do anything! Behavior is determined by thoughts, interpretations and perceptions
- Are your perceptions always accurate (remember the physiological changes in your body are the same for fear and excitement)
- What use does BLAME serve?
- What is the difference between BLAME and RESPONSIBILITY?
- Is it ok to be WRONG?   IMPERFECT?   i.e. 'Human'
- Can you differentiate between -Fact; Opinion; Emotional Response
- Avoid comparing yourself to others…there will always be people who are better than you and worse than you in any given area…NO ONE IS PERFECT AT EVERYTHING!!(or anything actually)

Accept yourself for who you are and what you are

I think I'm cool!

Remember everyone's goals are or should be basically:

- Be happy
- Do no harm to yourself
- Do no harm to others

You do not need to be like everyone else as long as you are safe, happy and allow others to be safe and happy around you (you really can wear odd socks)

Do not label yourself (or others). Avoid put downs and negative judgments/ Words are powerful: Make sure your self-talk is positive and encouraging

Learn to reduce your anxiety – FEAR feeds low confidence and depression

Make time to have fun and enjoy life, give yourself permission to be happy!

Treat yourself to a new do!

Be Nice to You!

Make a list of your achievements and keep adding to it!

- Write down the things you (and/or other's) like about you
- Discover your skills/talents (yes you do have some) – then use them frequently
- Learn to accept compliments
- Stop feeling you have to justify yourself to everyone

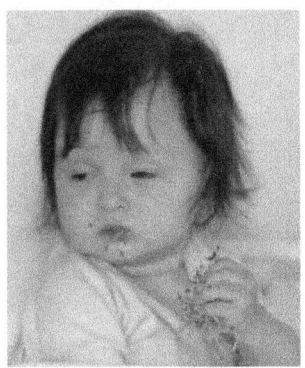

'My Mum loves me just the way I am'

Create a 'Master List of My Qualities'
Nothing is more attractive than confidence!

List EVERYTHING positive or good you can think of about yourself.
List EVERYTHING negative or bad you can think of about yourself

How do you put yourself down?
How do you positively reinforce yourself?
What does this tell you about your self-esteem and what can you do about it?

What can you do to build your inner strength and confidence? Chances are a lot of people (including yourself) put a lot of time and effort into lowering your self-esteem. Even other kids, when you were at school, helped destroy your self-esteem without even knowing or caring who you were…it was how you interpreted their words and their behavior. .

So How Do I Fix It ????

(Re-read this book!)

Looking after yourself as though you were someone you cared about!

Express your emotions and opinions…as though you actually had a right to…

Work on your self-talk…Acknowledge when you do something even half right…acknowledge your efforts…if you MUST compare…how about looking at the other end of the scale for a change…

Avoidance is OK in the short term!!
Desensitization and Rational Thinking are longer term tools!!

Remember in life there will always be some people who are better and some people who are not as good as you at any given time…The average person is after all just AVERAGE.

Find your purpose
Write down the ten
most valued aspects in
your life:
WHERE ARE YOUR
PRIORITIES?
What have you
discovered about
yourself and your
values?

"The Little Book & CD" series.

 Your Child the Little Scientist

 The Little Book to Revive Relationships

 The Little Book to Annihilate Anxiety

 The Little Book to Push Through Pain

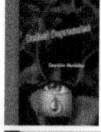 The Little Book to Defeat Depression

 The Little Book to Salvage Self Esteem

 The Little Book to be Physically Phabulous

 Amazing Abilities of your Magical Mind

CD therapy

Anxiety   Alcohol

Drugs   Depression

Smoking   Self Esteem

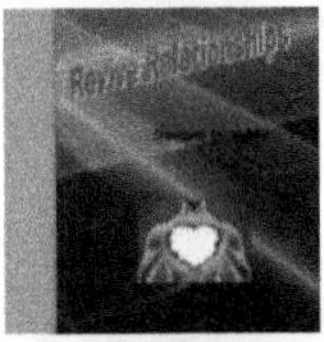

Relationships   Pain

Abandonment   Sleep

Anger   Health

 Magical Mind

Bibliography

Albert Ellis (1995)*Clinical Applications of Rational-Emotive Therapy*

Albert Ellis (1995) *Handbook of Cognitive Therapy Techniques*

Elizabeth Hills (2006) Getting in touch with your inner bitch,

Jon Kabat-Zinn, (2008)Full Catastrophe Living

MacKay & Fanning (2002) Self Esteem

Manual J Smith (2000) When I say No I feel Guilty

Michael J Free (1999) Cognitive therapy in groups*: Guidelines and resources in practice*

Rudolph Dreikurs (1985) Happy Children

Sat Chuen Hon, (1999) The Tao of Breath

Illustrations & Photography (2012) Friends 7 Family. Amanda Hockley. Istockphotos.com: Fotolia.

Myke Ashley Cooper: (Page 10) Cartoon used with the permission and generosity of the author.

THE AUTHOR

Denisia Hockley
Clinical Psychologist/Psychotherapist/Author
Dip.Psy.,BA.,BSc.(Hon)Masters Mental Health (Psychotherapy)
Registered AHPRA: (Australia): MAPS Clinical College (Australia)
Member APS (American Pain Society)
Member Association of Independent Authors USA
www.littlebookseries.us
littlebooks2013@gmail.com

Denisia J. Hockley is an Australian Clinical Psychologist: Since 1998 she has worked with everything from general anxiety and depression to victims of trauma and abuse to everyday families struggling with typical life issues as well as those with clinical psychiatric disorders. In 2010 she worked in California specializing in clients with chronic pain issues. As a therapist, she has worked in outback aboriginal settlements, men's correctional facilities, addictions programs and private practice/s. Her style is laidback informal, and solution-focused. As well as CBT, Psycho-education and other general practices she is a qualified psychotherapist and also works with Prof. Leon Petchkovsky with his Neuro feedback clinic. An ex-policewoman, she has had a colorful and diverse career. Denisia's specialties include Complex Post Traumatic Stress Disorder (CPTSD) & Developmental Trauma (non-organic) in adults and adolescents: which result in anxieties, depression, personality disorders, relationship and self-concept difficulties as well as many physiological symptoms including pain and gastrointestinal disorders.

She is most passionate and fascinated by brain science and as she terms it... The Amazing Abilities of our Magical Minds, She has written a number of book including *Your Child the Little Scientist:* Her Little Book Series address every aspect of life, health, happiness, and mental wellbeing and can be obtained as E-Books at www.littlebookseries.us She also has a series of CD therapies covering Sleep/Addiction/Health & Weight/Anxiety/Depression and more: Visit her site for more information on these.